Hairstyles Coloring Book - No' 2

Women Models With Beautiful Hair Designs For Girls, Teenagers & Adults

Rachel Mintz

Images used under license from Shutterstock.com

Copyright © 2018 Palm Tree Publishing - All rights reserved.
No part of this publication may be reproduced, distributed, or transmitted in any form or by any means, including photocopying, recording, or other electronic or mechanical methods, without the prior written permission of the publisher, except in the case of brief quotations embodied in critical reviews and certain other noncommercial uses permitted by copyright law.

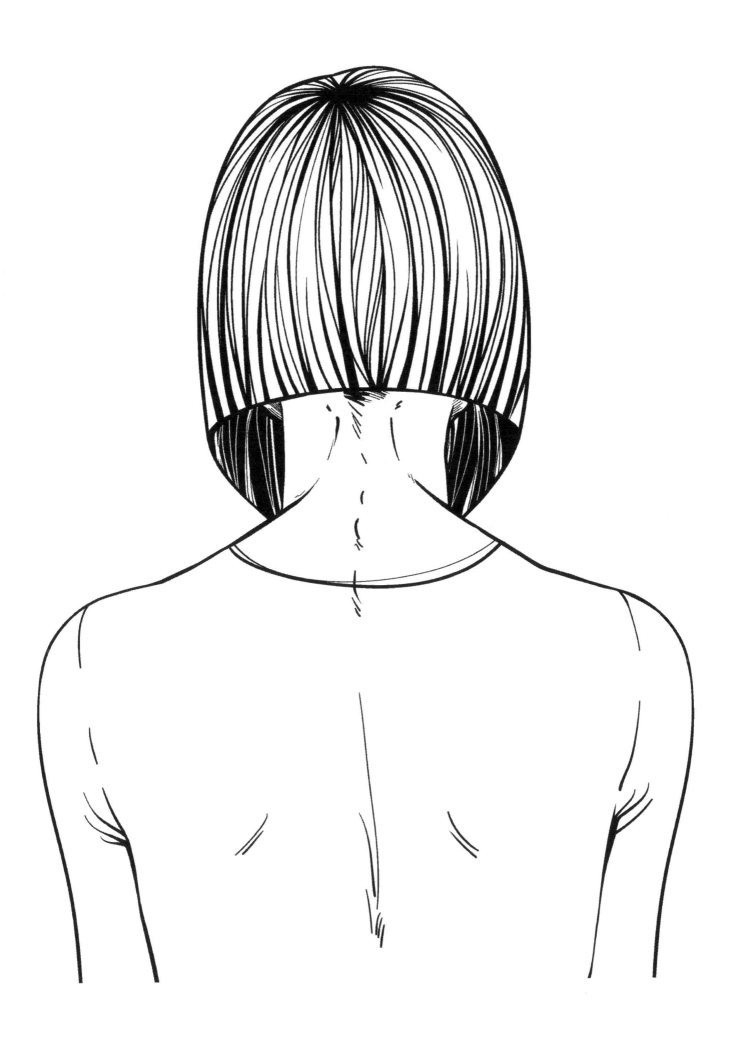

Thank you for coloring with us

Please consider to rate & review

More from our coloring books:

Thank you for coloring with us

Please consider to rate & review

Made in the USA
Columbia, SC
02 January 2019